D0783558

Published and distributed by
TOBAR LIMITED
The Old Aerodrome, Worlingham, Beccles,
Suffolk, NR34 7SP, UK
www.tobar.co.uk

This edition printed 2009

© 2006 Arcturus Publishing Limited

Printed in China

ISBN: 978-1-903230-27-5

INTRODUCTION

From plaintiffs to judges, lawyers to defendants, they say that everyone has their day in court. Well, judging from some of the exchanges and stories in this book, some people should be kept away from the courtroom!

Here we take a peek at the amusing exchanges and baffling civil cases that certainly make the jobs of judges and juries a lot harder (not to mention their task of keeping a straight face throughout the silly proceedings). You'll also be swept away by some of the rather huge payouts that defy

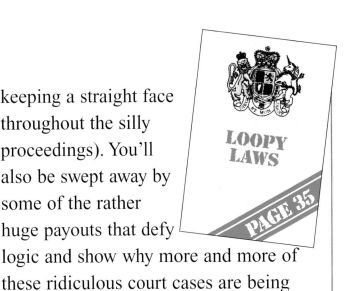

LOOPY LAWS PAGE 35

logic and show why more and more of these ridiculous court cases are being filed!

OUTRAGEOUS OUTCOMES PAGE 55

So, silence in court and no sniggering at the back – the law is a really serious business… a seriously funny business that is!

CRAZY CIVIL CASES

Here's proof that everyone wants to blame somebody else for anything that ever goes wrong… ever. That sound like a mouthful? Well, wait until you read some of the trumped-up nonsense that has been presented in court! Some people are not happy to take responsibility for their own actions, and instead will try all manner of ridiculous ways and means to shift the blame to someone else – whether that is an individual, a huge company, or someone that appears at face value to have no connection to the case at all. Then they sue for stupid amounts of money, although they are often left somewhat red-faced by the outcome.

To accompany this chapter, where logic has clearly given way to insanity (and lashings of greed), we'll take a look at those who have taken to the stand but who never managed to hit the jackpot because, quite frankly, their IQs were simply not up to it under cross-examination!

Petrol station staff in the dog house!

Exhibit A

The victims of a drink-driving accident were not just content with suing the drunk driver Brian Lee Tarver – they also decided to sue the petrol station that sold $3 worth of petrol to Tarver shortly before the head-on crash that seriously injured the two victims.

Lawyers argued that Tarver would have run out of petrol before the crash had the petrol station not provided him with more fuel. They said that, although staff at the petrol station could not have prevented Tarver from getting behind the wheel of a car, they should have refused to sell him petrol.

The Tennessee Supreme Court ruled that the case could go forward…

Fancy indulging in a crazy civil case of your own? Well, if you want to stand any chance of hitting the jackpot in court, we recommend that you don't behave like the defendants and witnesses featured in the excerpts here...

Question: Did the lady standing at the driveway subsequently identify herself to you?

Answer: Yes, she did.

Question: Who did she say she was?

Answer: She said she was the owner of the dog's wife.

———O———

Question: Did you ever stay all night with this man in New York?

Answer: I refuse to answer that question.

Question: Did you ever stay all night with this man in Chicago?

Answer: I refuse to answer that question.

Question: Did you ever stay all night with this man in Miami?

Answer: No.

———O———

Question: Are you married?

Answer: No, I'm divorced.

Question: And what did your husband do before you divorced him?

Answer: A lot of things I didn't know about.

Exhibit A

God sues magicians

Exhibit A

One cannot help but be sceptical of Christopher Roller's chances of success in court, seeing as the basis for his suit is that he is God. Still, stranger things have happened. Mr Roller is suing magicians David Blaine and David Copperfield because he cannot understand how they perform their tricks.

He is demanding that they either reveal their secrets to him or pay him 10% of their lifelong earnings (a figure which he estimates at around $50 million). The basis for his crazy case is that the performers defy the laws of physics and must therefore be using "godly powers".

Since Roller believes that he is God, he argues that the magicians must be stealing his power, hence the dubious lawsuit…

Question: Are you saying the witness is lying about witnessing you performing the robbery?

Answer: Yes.

Question: What makes you say that?

Answer: Because she wasn't there when I did it.

———O———

Question: Did you tell your lawyer that your husband had offered you indignities?

Answer: He didn't offer me nothing; he just said I could have the furniture.

———O———

Question: Your foster son, Corey, who cooks for him?

Answer: Oh, I do.

Question: How often do you cook for him?

Answer: We have probably one good meal a week.

Exhibit A

Question: Well, no commentary on your cooking, but how many 'bad' meals do you have?

———O———

Question: So, you are unconscious, and they pulled you from the bucket. So what happened then?

Answer: Mr Stewart then gave me artificial insemination, you know, mouth-to-mouth.

Location, location, location

Exhibit A

When New Yorker Tanisha Torres received her mobile phone bill from Radio Shack, she was appalled to see that her address had been written as 'Crimedanch' rather than the correct 'Wyndanch'. A local in-joke, Wyndanch is often referred to as Crimedanch due to its rather high crime rate.

However, Ms Torres did not see the funny side and, rather than talking to the people at Radio Shack and explaining the problem, she decided to sue them for unspecified damages. "I'm not a criminal," explained Ms Torres. "My son plays on the high school football team." Ms Torres also claimed she suffered "outrage" and "embarrassment", despite the fact that she and the post office staff were the only people to see the letter.

Exhibit A

Question: Did he pick the dog up by the ears?

Answer: No.

Question: What was he doing with the dog's ears?

Answer: Picking them up in the air.

Question: Where was the dog at this time?

Answer: Attached to the ears.

Question: Miss, were you cited in the accident?

Answer: Yes sir – I was so 'cited, I peed all over myself!

Question: Do you drink when you're on duty?

Answer: I don't drink when I'm on duty, unless I come on duty drunk.

Exhibit A

Lawyer is reptile?

Exhibit A

Lawyers have been called many things, but be careful of calling one a reptile – or else you may well find yourself in the dock! California attorney Linda Ross sued when her business was listed in the Yellow Pages under the heading 'Reptiles'. The mistake had been made when the company behind the Yellow Pages, GTE Directories, did not update their records (as Ms Ross's number had previously belonged to a business called Reptile Show).

Asking for $100,000, Ms Ross claimed that the misplacing of her ad had left her open to "a great many jokes and hostile phone calls, hissing as she walks by and other forms of ridicule". By drawing the case to the public's attention, Ms Ross has also been ridiculed by newspapers and Jay Leno on *The Tonight Show*.

She also admits that her mother "laughed for ten minutes" when she found out about the case...

Question: Mrs. Jones, is your appearance this morning pursuant to a deposition notice that I sent to your attorney?

Answer: No. This is how I dress when I go to work.

———○———

Question: What is your brother-in-law's name?

Answer: Borofkin.

Question: What's his first name?

Answer: I can't remember.

Question: He's been your brother-in-law for years, and you can't remember his first name?

Answer: No. I tell you I'm too excited. [Rising from the witness chair and pointing to Mr Borofkin] Nathan, for God's sake, tell them your first name!

———○———

Question: What is your name?

Answer: Ernestine McDowell.

Question: And what is your marital status?

Answer: Fair.

Exhibit A

Exhibit A

Shifting the blame

The case of Caesar Barber is one that truly shows how ridiculous court case culture has become. Mr Barber, a resident of New York City, is 56 years old and weighs 270 pounds. He is obese, diabetic and suffers from heart disease. He claimed that he allowed his body to get into this state through no fault of his own.

Instead, he sued fast food restaurants KFC, McDonald's, Burger King and Wendy's, claiming that they had 'forced' him to eat in their establishments four or five times a week. It was also their fault, stated Mr Barber, because they didn't tell him that their food was fattening and not good for him. Fortunately, some sense prevailed and the judge threw the case out twice and banned it from being filed again.

Question: And who is this person you are speaking of?

Answer: My ex-widow said it.

―――――○―――――

Exhibit A

Question: Mrs Smith, do you actually believe that you are emotionally unstable?

Answer: I used to be.

Question: How many times have you committed suicide?

Answer: Four times.

―――――○―――――

Question: So, after the anaesthesia, when you came out of it, what did you observe with respect to your scalp?

Answer: I didn't see my scalp the whole time I was in the hospital.

Question: It was covered?

Answer: Yes, bandaged.

Question: Then, later on, what did you see?

Answer: I had a skin graft. My buttocks were removed and put on top of my head.

Jumped-up charges

Exhibit A

A crazy trend called 'garage jumping' has led one teenager's family to sue the city of Orlando, Florida. The trend involves jumping from one multi-storey car park to another. Sadly, Tim Bargfrede was somewhat unsuccessful when trying to follow his friends jumping, and fell six floors.

He survived the fall, but his family claim that he was not to blame, and that the city of Orlando should have done more to prevent 'garage jumping' from happening.

The Bargfrede family have also decided to sue the owner of one of the car parks, claiming that the fence was simply not high enough to prevent their dimwitted son from making his ill-fated jump.

Question: How did you happen to go to Dr Cherney?

Answer: Well, a gal down the road had had several of her children by Dr Cherney, and said he was really good.

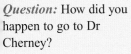

The Court: In this case, the request is made for the appointment of the psychologist for the performance of an IQ test. The court does not see the need for an IQ test since it appears to me that he is dumber than a fencepost.

Counsel: Has the court stated it in numerical terms?

The Court: His IQ is less than zero.

Question: Can you describe what the person who attacked you looked like?

Answer: No. He was wearing a mask.

Question: What was he wearing under the mask?

Answer: Err... his face.

Exhibit A

Exhibit A

The bottom line

Humiliation now comes with a price tag, according to one woman who is suing a circus after an embarrassing incident occurred when she was in the audience of one of their shows. The woman, who is asking for an undisclosed amount, was sat in the front row during the show and a dancing horse was performing in front of her. Something caused the horse to take a few steps back and "while in this situation, the horse evacuated his bowels into her lap". Doubtlessly an unpleasant experience, and as it "occurred in full view of many people… all of who laughed at the occurrence", it caused the lady in question "much embarrassment, mortification, and mental pain and suffering".

Goodness knows what repeating the whole experience in a court of law is going to do to the poor, poor woman!

The Court: You may call your next witness.

Defendant's Attorney: Your Honour, at this time I would like to swat [the opposing counsel] on the head with his client's deposition.

The Court: You mean read it?

Defendant's Attorney: No, sir. I mean to swat him on the head with it. Pursuant to Rule 32, I may use the deposition "for any purpose" and that's the purpose I want to use it for.

The Court: Well, it does say that.

[There is a quiet pause.]
The Court: There being no objection, you may proceed.

Defendant's Attorney: Thank you, Judge.

[Thereafter, defendant's attorney swats plaintiff's attorney on the head with the deposition.]

Exhibit A

Plaintiff's Attorney (the victim): But Judge ...

The Court: Next witness.

Plaintiff's Attorney: We object.

The Court: Sustained. Next witness.

Truly distressing…

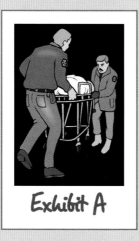

Exhibit A

Janice Bird took her mother Nita to a Los Angeles County hospital in 1994 for surgery. However, something went wrong during the procedure and Nita Bird was rushed into emergency surgery. In 2002, the court heard how Janice and her sister (who'd arrived at the hospital later) had suffered emotional distress.

Unbelievably, the sisters were suing the doctors because they had witnessed their mother "being rushed down the hallway" into emergency surgery and this had caused them emotional distress. Fortunately, common sense prevailed, although the case made it all the way to the California Supreme Court before the court ruled against the sisters.

The Court: Is there any reason why you couldn't serve as a juror in this particular case?

Potential Juror: I don't want to be away from my job that long.

The Court: Can't they do without you at work?

Potential Juror: Yes, but I don't really want them to know that.

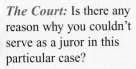

Question: Tell me what you were like from age 17 to the present. What have your feelings been about having kids?

Answer: I wanted to pursue an education and then meet the perfect person and be married a couple of years, save some money, buy a house, and start a family.

Question: When did that change?

Answer: It didn't.

Question: I think we all realize that as we get older, we're not going to marry the perfect person.

Answer: My wife did.

Question: Have you ever heard of Sigmund Freud?

Answer: Yes. He lives in Las Vegas.

Question: I think you're thinking of Siegfried and Roy, aren't you? But Sigmund Freud was actually a little older than that...

Exhibit A

The joke's on them

Exhibit A

Bob Dougherty was the victim of a practical joke when some prankster put glue on the toilet seat inside the public toilets of a Home Depot shop in Louisville, Colorado. Dougherty was stuck to the seat and, understandably, humiliated and upset. However, he reasonably conceded that this was the work of an outside joker and "not Home Depot's fault".

Despite this, the store offered Mr Dougherty $2,000 – at which point Mr Dougherty's reason seemed to desert him.

Rather than accept the payment graciously, he deemed the amount "insulting" and filed a suit against Home Depot, asking for three million dollars...

Defendant: Judge, I want you to appoint me another lawyer.

Judge: And why is that?

Defendant: Because the Public Defender isn't interested in my case.

Judge (addressing the Public Defender): Do you have any comments on the defendant's motion?

Public Defender: I'm sorry, Your Honour. I wasn't listening.

Exhibit A

Question: Are you going to be generally discussing that issue?

Answer: If asked a question about it, yes.

Question: Have you, in your mind, thought of a question that might be asked that you're going to offer an opinion on? I'm not going to throw stones into the wind trying to guess what you're going to say.

———O———

Question: How old is your son, the one living with you?

Answer: 38 or 35, I can't remember which.

Question: How long has he lived with you?

Answer: 45 years.

Godfather's grudge

Exhibit A

James Brown – also known as the Godfather of Soul – has had an eventful life and been on the wrong side of the law several times. However, public sympathy may be with Brown on this occasion.

Two of the singer's daughters, Deanna Brown Thomas and Yamma Brown Lumar, have sued their father for more than $1 million, saying that he holds a grudge against them and has sworn to the press that they will "never get a dime" from him.

Furthermore, Deanna and Yamma claim that their father owes them royalties on more than 20 of his hit songs which they claim to have helped him write. All of which could be considered reasonable, except for the fact that in 1976 – when Brown was riding high in the charts with *Get Up Offa That Thing* (one of the songs named in the case) – his daughters were aged three and six.

Question: What was the first thing your husband said to you when he woke that morning?

Answer: He said, "Where am I, Cheryl?"

Question: And why did that upset you?

Answer: My name is Kathy.

Question: You are aware that you are here on charges of driving without a licence?

Answer: Yes.

Question: Do you have a driving licence?

Answer: No.

Question: How did you get to court this morning?

Answer: I drove.

Question: Sir, what is your IQ?

Answer: Well, I think I can see pretty good.

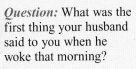

Exhibit A

Question: And you check your radar unit frequently?

Answer: Yes, sir, I do.

Question: And was your radar unit functioning correctly at the time you had the plaintiff on radar?

Answer: Yes, sir, it was malfunctioning correctly.

Exhibit A

Exhibit A

A devil of a lawsuit

An unnamed plaintiff decided to sue Satan for the violation of his civil rights. The plaintiff claimed that Satan had caused him misery on numerous occasions, as well as deliberately placing obstacles in his path that ensured his downfall and – as a result of this – had also led to him being denied his constitutional rights.

Before dismissing the case the judge commented: "We question whether the plaintiff may obtain personal jurisdiction over the defendant in this judicial district… the plaintiff has failed to include with his complaint the required form of instructions for the United States Marshal for directions as to service of process." Quite why the plaintiff was not arrested for wasting everyone's time is another relevant question…

Question: Do you know if your daughter has ever been involved in Voodoo or the occult?

Answer: We both do.

Question: Voodoo?

Answer: We do.

Question: You do?

Answer: Yes. Voodoo.

———○———

Question: Officer, when you stopped the defendant, were your red and blue lights flashing?

Answer: Yes.

Question: Did the defendant say anything to you when she got out of her car?

Answer: Yes, sir.

Question: What did she say to you?

Answer: She said, "What disco am I at?"

———○———

Question: Did you blow your horn or anything?

Answer: After the accident?

Question: Before the accident.

Answer: Sure, I played for ten years. I even went to school for it.

Exhibit A

Nailing the problem

Exhibit A

Ann Laerzio's visit to the Octavia salon in 2001 ended up in a $500,000 lawsuit. Ms Laerzio called in to have her acrylic fingernail repaired at a cost of $5.

However, she claims that the nail technician cut her finger during the repair, which then became infected. As a result she was "forced to undergo multiple surgeries, has had her nail removed and now has a permanent disfigurement."

Her attorney admits, "the $500,000 figure isn't necessarily what we'll get in court. It's to put some attention on the case, and to show how important we consider it. There has been at least one surgery because of it and there may have to be more."

A bolt from the blue

Being hit by lightning would be seen by many as a classic act of God, for which no individual or company could be held responsible. Right? Well, think again. "That would be a lot of people's knee-jerk reaction in these

Exhibit A

types of situations," claims the lawyer for Shawn Perkins. Mr Perkins, from Laurel, Indiana, was unfortunate enough to be struck by lightning while in the car park at King's Island amusement park in Mason, Ohio.

He decided that this was the fault of the amusement park and proceeded to sue them for an undisclosed amount. His argument (for those who are still sticking to that 'act of God' defence) was that the amusement park should have warned him that it was dangerous to be outside during a thunderstorm.

Out of order

They may look silly in their wigs and garish red robes but when you read this following exchange between a judge and a defendant, you have to admire the court's patience...

Question: Please repeat after me, "I swear by Almighty God..."

Answer: I swear by Almighty God.

Question: That the evidence that I give...

Answer: That's right.

Question: Repeat it.

Answer: Repeat it.

Question: No! Repeat what I said.

Answer: What you said when?

Question: That the evidence that I give...

Answer: That the evidence that I give.

Question: Shall be the truth and...

Answer: It will, and nothing but the truth!

Question: Please. Just repeat after me, "Shall be the truth and..."

Answer: I'm not a scholar, you know.

Question: We can appreciate that. Just repeat after me, "Shall be the truth and..."

Answer: Shall be the truth and.

Question: Say, "Nothing..."

Answer: Okay. [The witness remains silent.]

Question: No! Don't say nothing. Say, "Nothing but the truth..."

Answer: Yes.

Question: Can't you say, "Nothing but the truth...?"

Answer: Yes.

Question: Well? Do so.

Answer: You're confusing me.

Question: Just say, "Nothing but the truth..."

Answer: Is that all?

Question: Yes.

Answer: Okay. I understand.

Question: Then say it.

Answer: What?

Question: "Nothing but the truth..."

Answer: But I do! That's just it.

Question: You must say, "Nothing but the truth..."

Answer: I will say nothing but the truth!

Question: Please, just repeat these four words: "Nothing. But. The. Truth."

Exhibit A

Answer: What? You mean, like, now?

Question: Yes, now! Please. Just say those four words.

Answer: "Nothing. But. The. Truth."

Question: Thank you.

Answer: I'm just not a scholar, you know.

"I'm no bimbo"

Exhibit A

The cartoon series *Stripperella* has become the subject of a lawsuit filed by former stripper Janet Clover of Palm Coast, Florida. Miss Clover is suing Viacom, Pamela Anderson and Stan Lee. Ms Anderson performs the voice of the lead character in *Stripperella*, while Mr Lee created the show. Or did he? According to Ms Clover, she came up with the premise of the show (a stripper who is also a superhero) and told Mr Lee about it when she was performing a private dance for him in a strip club.

However, when asked by a newspaper for more details, Ms Clover could only come up with: "I can't remember much about Mr Lee, little bits and pieces come back. You know, I meet a lot of men." However, Ms Clover was insistent that she wanted *Stripperella* "off TV because it's not his idea... He's going to know I'm not just a bimbo." Anderson, Lee and Viacom have yet to comment on the case.

LOOPY LAWS

We live in the 21st century. We are a civilized people (well, sort of). We don't live in a police state (stop sniggering at the back). We have serious issues to worry about such as the future of our planet. So why, oh why, are there such ridiculous laws still on the books in countries the world over?

Don't believe us? Then cast an eye over the next chapter and you'll wonder how we've all managed to make it this far! From the US's legal system with its weird and wonderful collection of ridiculous laws to Singapore's draconian decrees, there's something here for everyone to run the risk of ending up in the slammer. And here in the UK, well, we seem to love banning things left, right and centre!

So, with such ridiculous laws plaguing the courts, you might have thought it would be very useful to have a lawyer who is able run rings round the court system. Well, judging from the legal eagles and their quotes, also featured throughout this chapter, you might end up having serious difficulty actually locating a decent one… so you may as well throw the towel in now!

Colorado, USA

Exhibit A

The Crime: The destruction of labels.

The Law: Citizens of Colorado live in fear that if they rip the tag from a pillow or mattress, they could be sent to jail. Sounds ridiculous but it's true – or was true. The powers-that-be recently conceded that the law was absurd and the Governor formalized its abolishment by gleefully tearing off a label in front of the press, stating: "I've been worrying about the mattress inspector jumping through the window for years…"

Georgia, USA

The Crime: The use of sex toys.

The Law: In modern society, sex toys are used by loving couples (or by frustrated people in moments of absolute desperation). Either way, in Georgia be careful when using something that goes buzz in the night – or it's time for court. Not convinced? Well, way back in 1968, a hot-under-the-collar citizen of Georgia was actually convicted for using a sex toy, and the very same law still remains on the state's books today.

With such silly laws wasting valuable court time, you would have thought it would be easy for any half-decent lawyer to defend their clients with ease. Well, think again because, judging from these crazy quotes, lawyers don't seem to be able to defend anything whatsoever...

Question: When was the last time you saw the deceased?

Answer: At his funeral.

Question: Did he make any comments to you at that time?

Question: And what did he do then?

Answer: He came home, and next morning he was dead.

Question: So when he woke up the next morning, he was dead?

Question: Now, doctor, isn't it true that when a person dies in his sleep, in most cases he just passes quietly away and doesn't know anything about it until the next morning?

Exhibit A

Finland

Exhibit A

The Crime: Not paying fees for playing music in your cab.

The Law: The cabbie's life is hard enough, what with drunks and fare dodgers raising merry hell on a typical Friday night in Finland. But now, the Finnish courts have muscled into make their lives even more miserable. To be allowed to play music in your cab in Finland while you are carrying passengers, you must pay royalties annually. Think this sounds preposterous and unenforceable? Well, you tell that to taxi driver Lauri Luotonen who found himself in front of a judge who told him to pay 22 Euros per year for each of the two years he had refused to cough up.

But perhaps we should pity ourselves the most – if this law ever comes to Britain, we could be forced to listen to the taxi driver rambling on even more about "the kids of today/the government/the price of fish."

Question (to the court): Now, as we begin, I must ask you to banish all present information from your minds, if you have any.

Question: She had three children, right?

Answer: Yes.

Question: How many were boys?

Answer: None.

Question: Were there girls?

Question: This Myasthenia Gavis, does it affect your memory at all?

Answer: Yes.

Question: And in what ways does it affect your memory?

Answer: I forget things.

Question: You forget things? Can you give us an example of something you've forgotten?

Exhibit A

Singapore

Exhibit A

The Crime: Pretty much anything to do with the humble car, it seems. No four wheels are safe!

The Laws: You don't want to own a car in Singapore. That's a fact. Never mind that for a Ford Focus you'll be looking to pay Porsche money thanks to the government's unique car tax scheme. But once you do have your pride and joy in your driveway, there are several 'issues' you will need to consider.

Firstly, you could find yourself on the wrong end of a fine if you should let your car get too filthy. Well, no one likes a dirty car but this draconian piece of legislation is made worse when you consider that using a hose to wash your car is also illegal.

Because most of Singapore's water is pumped in from Malaysia, the government decided that it was best to introduce conservation laws and save some money in the process.

Once your car is legally spick and span, your woes don't stop there. Do be sure that you never drive the car out of the country with your petrol tank less than three quarters full.

The reason is simple – petrol just over the border in Malaysia costs half the amount it does in Singapore and the Singaporean government doesn't want valuable income pouring out of the country. Those who do find themselves running on fumes as they head across the border can expect a rather hefty fine of well over £1,500.

With such stinging anti-car policies in place, we heartily recommend that if you are considering moving to Singapore, stick with their really rather excellent public transport system instead.

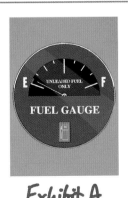

Exhibit A

Greece

The Crime: To be caught playing videogames in public.

The Law: This law was born out of the public's concern – but its execution has been utterly ridiculous. At the heart of the bizarre decree was an attempt to put a stop to illegal gambling after members of a political party were filmed having a flutter in an illegal gambling den.

Exhibit A

Enter the new law to stop such skulduggery. Alas, the new law also meant that all electronic gaming (even playing chess on the net in the comfort of your own home) became outlawed. The government appeared to find it impossible to tell the difference between Sonic the Hedgehog and an unlawful game of poker.

There was uproar all over the European Union and the government amended the law in 2002. However, it was still illegal to play videogames in internet cafes and in 2004, 80 computers were seized from cafes in Greece, and arrests made. The law has now fallen into such ill repute that it has been suspended.

Question: Did he kill you?

Question: How long have you been French Canadian?

Exhibit A

Question: Can you describe the individual?

Answer: He was about medium height and had a beard.

Question: Was this a male or a female?

Question: Were you present in court this morning when you were sworn in?

Exhibit A

Question: So you were gone until you returned?

New Jersey

Exhibit A

The Crime: Pumping your own petrol.

The Law: Best not to hop out and start to fill up your car's petrol tank if you should be visiting New Jersey – or else you could find yourself with a fine. After all, you must by law let the workers at any petrol station in the state fill up the car for you.

The reason? Well, some say that by getting attendants to do the dirty work it actually brings down the insurance cost for the garage; after all, there is less chance of a member of public accidentally igniting themselves while filling their car up. Which, judging from the mass of headlines we have never seen detailing such incidents, doesn't happen at all.

The other explanation for sticking with mandatory attendants is much more simple and perhaps more cynical – it helps pump up employment figures…

Question: Does Quicken have – strike that. Did the Quicken program that you acquired have a capacity to generate a financial statement?

Answer: Yes.

Question: Was Quicken a – was the Quicken program that you – when did you – I'm sorry. Let me start over. When was the Quicken program first acquired?

Answer: January 1st of 1992.

Question: I don't know what I'd do if I weren't so articulate. It really has been the key to my success so far...

———◯———

Question: Were you alone or by yourself?

———◯———

Question: How far apart were the vehicles at the time of the collision?

———◯———

Question: I understand you're Bernie Davis's mother.

Answer: Yes.

Question: How long have you known him?

Exhibit A

The legal profession's fall from grace has been quite spectacular thanks to their ludicrous lawsuits. So we recommend that you arm yourself with the following jokes so, if you are ever unfortunate enough to meet a lawyer, you can let them know exactly what you think of them.

What's the difference between God and a lawyer?

God doesn't think he's a lawyer.

You are in a room with a mass murderer, a terrorist and a lawyer. You have a gun with only two bullets. What do you do?

Shoot the lawyer twice.

Do you know what lawyers and sperm have in common?

It takes 300,000 of them to make one human being.

Why is it that many lawyers have broken noses?

Exhibit A

From chasing parked ambulances.

———○———

What's the difference between a lawyer and a vampire?

A vampire only sucks blood at night.

———○———

What are lawyers good for?

They make used car salesmen look good.

———○———

What did the lawyer name his daughter?

Sue.

———○———

How can you tell when your lawyer is lying?

His lips move.

Exhibit A

How many lawyers does it take to screw in a light bulb?

Three. One to climb up the ladder, one to shake the ladder and then the other one to sue the ladder company.

———○———

Why won't a shark attack a lawyer swimming in the ocean?

Professional courtesy.

Arizona, USA

The Crime: Hunting camels.

The Law: It's one of those double-take laws – can you imagine a redneck armed with a rifle killing a rare animal not indigenous to the country? It may sound absurd but there is a flicker of truth to it. Back in the mid-1800s, the US army decided that it might be an interesting experiment to bring over camels to the States to see if the humble camel could be used to transport soldiers and army stock. Alas, the bloody Civil War ended these ambitious plans.

Exhibit A

Plucky business types though reckoned that the camels could still be used for delivering goods to mining communities in states like Arizona. But, due to a combination of issues, the camel never really caught on and in 1913 Arizona declared them officially extinct from the state. However, fast forward to the 1950s and hunters were still reporting sightings of our humped friend in the desert.

Whether there is a current law still in place to guard these errant camels is open to much dispute – but perhaps if you look hard enough, if you can find them, you can hire the… ex-military Camel Corps!

Question: Was it you or your brother that was killed in the war?

Question: At the time you first saw Dr McCarty, had you ever seen him prior to that time?

Question: Was that the same nose you broke as a child?

Question: Now, Mrs Johnson, how was your first marriage actually terminated?

Answer: By death.

Question: And by whose death was it terminated?

Exhibit A

Exhibit A

Banned in the UK!

Exhibit A

It's a dark, dangerous world out there – and not for the reasons you might be thinking. No, in the UK, windows, rambling and even teddy bears could mean the difference between life and death according to the politically correct.

One primary school in London has banned the children's game Daisy Chains for fear of spreading germs via hand contact. Meanwhile, students at a school in Gloucestershire have been told they must not open windows just in case they accidentally slip out and plummet to their deaths. As you do.

The madness continues – teddy bears have been accused of being too cuddly to offer as prizes because they may encourage children to gamble and even the humble flower has come in for some flack – Cheltenham council told its residents that flowers should not be planted under trees for fear that such an action may cause a sprained wrist. Who needs laws when we have political correctness? God forbid.

Question: You don't know what it was, and you didn't know what it looked like, but can you describe it?

Exhibit A

Question: You say that the stairs went down to the basement?

Answer: Yes.

Question: And these stairs, did they go up also?

Question: So, if I hit the prosecutor at this very moment and he fell over the back of this railing, hit his head and a subdural haematoma immediately began to form, the blood that was leaking into the space would have essentially the same components as the blood leaking into his teeny little brain?

Exhibit A

Singapore

The Crime: Being found naked in your own home.

Exhibit A

The Law: Pity anyone who should be so bold as to walk round in their birthday suit while at home. In Singapore, the heartland of uptight laws, being caught in the buff inside your own house is actually illegal because it is considered to be a form of pornography… so keep your (hot) pants on at all times.

The Crime: Chewing gum.

The Law: It's a great urban legend that to be caught chewing gum in public while in Singapore will mean facing years in a dark, dank prison being flogged three times a day. This fortunately is tittle-tattle – in Singapore, you may chew gum but shops are banned from selling it and, if you are found buying it, only then is it time for Mr Handcuffs. And woe betide the person who spits out their gum – there is only one place for spent gum and that's in the bin.

For Wrigley's addicts though, you are able to bring two packs of gum into the country with you – any more will be confiscated and don't be surprised if you find yourself fined for putting their customs through such a harrowing experience of handling a pack of extra chewy gum…

Exhibit A

So where has Singapore's hang-up with chewing gum come from? It is believed that the government got rather upset with youngsters using gum to mess up the doors of their high speed trains which resulted in delays and disruption for commuters. And as ever with Singaporean law, why use a softly-softly approach to cure one of society's ills when you can wield a sledgehammer…

Exhibit A

Urban Law or Urban Legend...?

... You decide with the following outrageous and ridiculous laws that are reportedly still on the law books in certain states across the US!

In Florida, men must never be spotted wearing any item that could be mistaken for a strapless gown.

In Massachusetts, goatees are banned by an old law which states that you must have paid a licence fee to sport one.

In Oklahoma, pull a face at a dog and you could find yourself in a federal 'dog house' for your rudeness.

In California, it is now illegal to stop kids from splashing about in puddles of water. Yep, folks, it's a very sorry day indeed when you have to legislate children's playtime...

OUTRAGEOUS OUTCOMES

Got debt problems? The bank manager breathing down your neck? That credit card company sending you nasty letters even though they were more than happy to let you slide steeply into debt in the first place? Well, never mind signing up with one of those all-in-one debt companies that plague daytime TV's advertising breaks – we recommend you sue. And sue big!

Yep, you can make squillions by throwing lawsuits at people left, right and centre! This chapter profiles some of the ridiculous civil actions that the people have brought in front of a judge – and against all the odds (and anything resembling common sense) have actually won! Who needs the lottery when you have the court system acting as a cash machine? Kerching!

And what the heck – if it doesn't go your way, you can always brush up on delivering a smart-assed answer or comment that you can hurl back at lawyers and judges to make you feel better. We've included a whole mass of classic quotes throughout this chapter as well to make sure that you at least win 'morally', if not hit the jackpot financially…

Exhibit A

That's the way the cookie crumbles...

Wanita Young won $900 when she sued two teenage girls for leaving cookies at her front door. The two girls had baked the cookies as a surprise for their neighbours and had left them outside houses with their lights still on, as the girls did not want to disturb anyone who was sleeping.

Ms Young claimed that seeing the shadowy figures outside her door caused her so much anxiety that she suffered a panic attack the next day. The $900 was awarded by a Colorado court for medical bills, although Ms Young was not awarded anything for pain and suffering.

Ms Young later said, "I'm not gloating about it. I just hope the girls learned a lesson."

With the public making money by running rings round the law, perhaps it's best to pay attention to the mischievous types who know how to bring the court to its knees. With laughter! And in the (due) process, ensuring that the court system is made to look even more ridiculous!

Question: Do you believe the defendant's plea of temporary insanity?

Answer: I don't buy temporary insanity as a murder defence. Because people kill people. That's an animal instinct. I think breaking into someone's home and then ironing all their clothes is temporary insanity.

Question: What can you tell us about the truthfulness and veracity of this defendant?

Answer: Oh, she will tell the truth. She said she'd kill that son-of-a-b***h – and she did!

Exhibit A

Question: Do you have any suggestions as to what prevented this from being a murder trial instead of an attempted murder trial?

Answer: The victim lived.

Exhibit A

Winners and losers

Just who were the winners in the class action lawsuit when two Texas auto insurers were accused of over-billing policy-holders back in 1985? The companies stood accused of over-billing their customers by around $100 million. The case came to court despite the state insurance regulators declaring that the companies' practice of rounding up their twice annual premiums up to the nearest dollar was actually legal.

In the end, the companies opted to settle the lawsuit and policy holders were treated to an astounding $5.50 each. It's safe to say that they were probably expecting more.

However, the lawyer who filed the suit did a little better – walking away with $8 million.

Question: Doctor, did you say he was shot in the woods?

Answer: No, I said he was shot in the lumbar region.

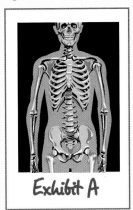

Exhibit A

Question: Doctor, how many autopsies have you performed on dead people?

Answer: All my autopsies have been performed on dead people.

Question: Are you sexually active?

Answer: No, I just lie there.

———O———

Question: Are you qualified to give a urine sample?

Answer: Yes, I have been since early childhood.

Exhibit A

It's good to be a lawyer

Exhibit A

Another case of winners also being losers happened when Oklahoma telephone company Southwestern Bell was sued for allegedly misrepresenting a service plan to six million customers. The lawyer who filed the lawsuit admitted that he could find little, if any, evidence of misconduct and the case was settled out of court to avoid horrifically high litigation costs.

However, the customers who felt they had been wrongly treated were merely awarded $15 credit; still a generous settlement in the minds of most people considering the case.

As for the lawyer who represented them, well, he would have been happy with his staggering $4 million in fees...

Question: And lastly, Gary, all your responses must be oral, okay? What school do you go to?

Answer: Oral.

Question: How old are you?

Answer: Oral.

Exhibit A

Question: Could you see him from where you were standing?

Answer: I could see his head.

Question: And where was his head?

Answer: Just above his shoulders.

Question: What is the meaning of sperm being present?

Answer: It indicates intercourse.

Question: Male sperm?

Answer: That is the only kind I know.

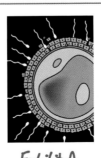

Exhibit A

Exhibit A

Too hot to handle

Stella Liebeck became a famous name when the Stella Awards – presented annually for ridiculous lawsuits – took their name from her infamous 1992 case against McDonald's. Ms Liebeck was 79 years old when she spilled a cup of McDonald's coffee in her lap while sat in the passenger seat of her grandson's car.

According to her attorneys, as a result of the spill, Ms Liebeck suffered severe burns over 6% of her body and had to undergo several skin grafts. She was also left with scarring on 15% of her body.

The case made the headlines across the world when she sued McDonald's and won her case. The fast food franchise subsequently had to shell out $2.9 million in damages. You could buy yourself a lot of Big Macs with that...

Question: Do you recall approximately the time that you examined that body of Mr Edington at the Rose Chapel?

Answer: It was in the evening. The autopsy started about 8:30 pm.

Question: And Mr. Edington was dead at the time, is that correct?

Answer: No, you idiot, he was sitting on the table wondering why I was doing an autopsy!

Exhibit A

Question: Please identify yourself for the record.

Answer: Colonel Ebenezer Jackson.

Question: What does the "Colonel" stand for?

Answer: Well, it's kinda like the "Honourable" in front of your name. Not a damn thing.

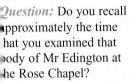

Question: When he went, had you gone and had she, if she wanted to and were able, for the time being excluding all the restraints on her not to go, gone also, would he have brought you, meaning you and she, with him to the station?

Answer: Objection. That question should be taken out and shot.

Blue moon

Exhibit A

The uncensored sight of University of Tennessee quarterback Peyton Manning mooning one of his fellow athletes in the training room was too much for one unnamed trainer who worked at the institution and witnessed the incident.

She claimed that the sight left her suffering 'psychological trauma' and the case was settled, with the trainer netting $300,000 for her 'pain'.

The university was – unsurprisingly – less than happy with the result and issued the following statement to the public to explain why they had made the settlement: "This payment is not an admission of guilt by the university or any other party and is a compromise of a disputed claim."

Exhibit A

Question: Now, in your report, you indicated that there is a minimum of cracking and no signs of settling.

Answer: Yes.

Question: When you say there is a minimum of cracking, I take it that you did find some cracking.

Answer: No. Because if I said there was no cracking, I would be in court just like this answering some stupid lawyers' questions. So I put minimum in there to cover myself, because somebody is going to find a crack somewhere.

Counsel: Move to strike the word "stupid," Your Honour.

———○———

Question: What gear were you in at the moment of impact?

Answer: Gucci sweats.

———○———

Question: Where was the location of the accident?

Answer: Approximately milepost 499.

Question: And where is milepost 499?

Answer: Probably between milepost 498 and 500.

A cut above the rest

Exhibit A

When Michelle Knepper decided that she wanted to undergo liposuction, she picked a doctor from the phone book. However, the doctor that she entrusted to perform the procedure was not a board qualified plastic surgeon but a dermatologist. When the inevitable complications arose, Mrs Knepper did what any outraged citizen would do – she sued.

But not the doctor – Mrs Knepper sued the company that printed the phone book, as the doctor's ad had not informed her that he was not qualified to perform the procedure. As ridiculous as this sounds, it pales in comparison to the $1.2 million she was awarded when her case came to court. And she wasn't the only one to benefit. Her husband also cashed in when he was awarded $375,000 for "loss of spousal services".

Question: Please state the location of your right foot immediately prior to impact.

Answer: Immediately before the impact, my right foot was located at the immediate end of my right leg.

———————○———————

Question: Then there's a minus $85,000 plus interest. What did you believe that referenced to when you signed it?

Answer: Creative financing.

Exhibit A

Exhibit A

Question: But if the discount wasn't on the sales order form or the invoice or the monthly print-out, where would it be?

Answer: In Kansas along with Dorothy and Toto.

Crime does pay

Exhibit A

A life of crime paid off for Terrence Dickson when he broke into a house while the family were away on their summer holiday. However, it wasn't the things he stole that made Mr Dickson his fortune. As he was exiting the house by way of the garage, Mr Dickson found himself trapped. The automatic garage door was not working, and the door between the house and the garage had locked when it closed.

Trapped in the garage for eight days, Mr Dickson survived by drinking cola and eating dry dog food. When he was 'rescued', Mr Dickson showed his criminal colours by suing the family whose home he had been attempting to rob, claiming the situation caused him undue mental anguish – and he won. The judge ordered the family to pay out $500,000 to Dickson.

Exhibit A

Question: And did the plaintiff tell you why she's feeling confident about going to trial in this case?

Answer: She says God's on her side.

Question: Any other reason other than that God's on her side?

Answer: She's telling the truth.

Question: Did you kill the victim?

Answer: No, I did not.

Question: Do you know what the penalties are for perjury?

Answer: Yes, I do. And they're a hell of a lot better than the penalty for murder.

Question: Doctor, as a result of your examination of the plaintiff, is the young lady pregnant?

Answer: The young lady is pregnant, but not as a result of my actual examination.

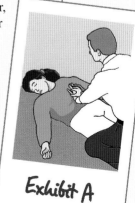

Exhibit A

Cruising out of control

Exhibit A

Seemingly rewarded for his stupidity, Mr Grazinski was driving home in his new 32ft Winnebago motor home. He joined the freeway and set the vehicle's cruise control at 70mph. He then left the wheel, went into the back of the vehicle and began to make himself a cup of coffee.

To no one's surprise except Mr Grazinski's, the Winnebago left the road and overturned into an embankment. Mr Graziski survived the crash and sued the Winnebago company, as his manual had not informed him that he should remain in his seat.

And of course, the jury agreed with him to the tune of $1.75 million and a brand spanking new Winnebago.

Question: Doctor, before you performed the autopsy, did you check for a pulse?

Answer: No.

Question: Did you check for blood pressure?

Answer: No.

Question: Did you check for breathing?

Answer: No.

Question: So then, it is possible that the patient was alive when you began the autopsy?

Answer: No.

Question: And how can you be so sure, Doctor?

Answer: Because his brain was sitting on my desk in a jar.

Question: But could the patient have still been alive nevertheless?

Answer: Yes, it is possible that he could have been alive and likely practising law somewhere.

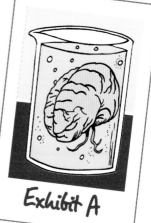

Exhibit A

Question: You are charged with habitual drunkenness. Have you anything to say in your defence?

Answer: Habitual thirstiness?

Cost of living

Exhibit A

When *The New York Times* reported that a woman received $14.1 million after being hit by a train, few people debated that she deserved some kind of compensation, although some folk thought the large figure was perhaps just a tad on the over-generous side.

However, it was then revealed in the police report that the woman in question had been trying to commit suicide at the time, and had been laying on the tracks in front of the train that hit her.

When this news hit, the award was reduced because of the woman's "comparative negligence". As a result of her failed suicide bid, the woman received a pilfering $9.9 million instead...

Exhibit A

Lawyer: How do you feel about defence attorneys?

Juror: I think they should all be drowned at birth.

Lawyer: Well, then, you are obviously biased for the prosecution.

Juror: That's not true. I think prosecutors should be drowned at birth too.

Defendant (after being given 90 days in jail): Can I address the court?

Judge: Of course.

Defendant: If I called you a son-of-a-b***h, what would you do?

Judge: I'd hold you in contempt and assess an additional five days in jail.

Defendant: What if I thought you were a son-of-a-b***h?

Judge: I can't do anything about that. There's no law against thinking.

Defendant: In that case judge, I think you're a son-of-a-b***h.

Doggone lawsuits!

Exhibit A

Joseph Shields and Thomas Rinks hit the headlines in 2003 when they sued the US fast food chain Taco Bell, claiming that the company had stolen their idea for an ad campaign featuring a talking Chihuahu: "It was a rollercoaster ride to get here, but we survived," said a clearly emotional and delighted Mr Rinks after the verdict was announced, "and a jury got to hear our story which is all we ever wanted from the beginning."

The two men – who claimed that Taco Bell breached payment on a contract regarding the dog idea, which they spent over a year developing – were awarded more than $30 million by the court.

Exhibit A

Question: Sir, did you actually see the accident?

Answer: Yes, sir.

Question: How far away were you when the accident happened?

Answer: 31 feet, six and one quarter inches.

Question: And how do you know it was exactly that distance?

Answer: Because when the accident happened, I took out a tape and measured it. I knew some stupid lawyer would ask me that question.

―――――○―――――

Question: Have you lived in this town all of your life?

Answer: Not yet.

―――――○―――――

Question: Now sir, I'm sure you are a very intelligent and honest man…

Answer: Thank you. If I weren't under oath, I'd return the compliment.

The following are actual statements placed on insurance forms where the car's driver attempted to summarize the details of their accident in the fewest words possible:

Exhibit A

Coming home I drove into the wrong house and collided with a tree I don't have.

The other car collided with my car without giving any warning of its intentions.

Exhibit A

I thought the window was down, but I found out it was up when I put my head through it.

A truck backed through my windshield and into my wife's face.

A pedestrian hit me and went under my car.

The guy was all over the road. I had to swerve a number of times before I hit him.

I pulled away from the side of the road, glanced at my mother-in-law, and then headed over an embankment.

In my attempt to kill a buzzing fly, I drove into a telephone pole.

I had been shopping for plants all day and was on my way home. As I reached an intersection, a hedge sprang up therefore obscuring my vision and I did not see the other car.

I had been driving for forty years when I fell

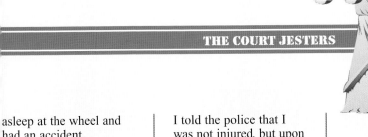

asleep at the wheel and had an accident.

———○———

The pedestrian had no idea which way to run, so I ran over him.

———○———

I was on my way to the doctor with rear end trouble when my universal joint gave way causing me to have an accident.

———○———

As I approached an intersection, a sign suddenly appeared in a place where no stop sign had ever appeared before. I was unable to stop in time to avoid the accident.

———○———

To avoid hitting the bumper of the car in front, I struck the pedestrian.

———○———

My car was legally parked as it backed into the other vehicle.

I told the police that I was not injured, but upon removing my hat, I found that I had a fractured skull.

———○———

I saw a slow moving, sad faced old gentleman as he bounced off the roof of my car.

———○———

The indirect cause of the accident was a little guy in a small car with a very big mouth.

———○———

I was thrown from my car as it left the road. I was later found in a ditch by some stray cows.

———○———

The telephone pole was approaching. I was attempting to swerve out of its way when it struck the front of my car.

———○———

Exhibit A

No laughing matter

Exhibit A

Jodee Berry is not a fan of practical jokes. So, when she won a toy doll in a competition instead of the Toyota that she had expected, she took the necessary steps to sue the company in charge of the contest. Waitresses at the Hooters restaurant in Panama City Beach had been told that the person who sold the most beer would win a Toyota. When Ms Berry won, she was blindfolded and led to the car park, where she came face to face with a toy Yoda from the *Star Wars* films.

Claiming breach of contract and fraudulent misrepresentation, Ms Berry quit her job and sued her former employers. Despite claiming that the contest was just an April Fools' joke, the restaurant settled the lawsuit and Ms Berry can now – says her lawyer – "pick out whatever type of Toyota she wants". Who's laughing now?